Super Baby Food Cookbook

Ruth Yaron

F. J. Roberts Publishing Company
Peckville, Pennsylvania

FIRST EDITION

Published by:
F. J. Roberts Publishing Company
20 Blythe Drive
Peckville, PA 18452
(815) 425-8942
www.SuperBabyFood.com

Printed in the United States of America

Publisher's Cataloging-In-Publication Data
(Prepared by The Donohue Group, Inc.)

Yaron, Ruth.
Super baby food cookbook / Ruth Yaron.

pages : illustrations, charts ; cm

ISBN: 978-0-9963000-2-5

1. Baby foods. 2. Infants—Nutrition. 3. Cookbooks. I. Title.

RJ216 .Y37 2015
641.5/6222

Design by Julie Murkette
Photo credits appear on page 150.

To Claudine Wolk and Julie Murkette,
without whom this book would not have been possible.

Disclaimer

Be sure to discuss with your baby's professional healthcare provider any food or drink before you feed it to your baby. This book contains information available only up to the copyright date. New information, or information contradicting that which is found in this book, should be actively sought from your child's competent healthcare professionals.

This book is sold with the understanding that neither F. J. Roberts Publishing, LLC, F. J. Roberts Holdings LLC, nor Ruth Yaron is engaged in rendering professional opinions or advice. If professional assistance is needed, the services of a competent healthcare provider, pediatrician, or registered dietitian should be sought. F. J. Roberts Publishing, LLC, F. J. Roberts Holdings LLC and/or Ruth Yaron shall have neither liability nor responsibility to any parent, person, or entity with respect to any illness, disability, injury, loss, or damage caused, or alleged to be caused, directly or indirectly by the information contained in this book.

Contents

Super Baby Food®

your complete guide to what, when, and how to feed your baby and toddler

OVER 350 YUMMY RECIPES · GREEN-BABY INFO
MONEY-SAVING TIPS · AND MUCH MORE

Introduction

My first book, *Super Baby Food*, originally published in 1996 and recently released in a revised and updated third edition, was a labor of love. The idea was simple. Teach parents how to feed their babies the best possible foods prepared at home with fresh ingredients in an easy way. The idea caught on. With over 25 printings and over 500,000 copies sold, *Super Baby Food* is more popular than ever. The only thing missing from "the big purple book" are pictures of the fantastic recipes included in it. With the *Super Baby Food Cookbook* we have come full circle.

I hope long-time fans will enjoy seeing their favorite super baby food recipes in full color and learn a few new tricks along the way as well. I hope newcomers to the Super Baby Food brand will learn how to feed their babies the very best and check out the latest *Super Baby Food*, still the "baby food bible," for additional information and guidance.

Overview of the *Super Baby Food* Diet

The *Super Baby Food Diet* is an extremely healthy diet composed of only whole, natural foods. It is based on these major components: whole grain cereals, vegetables and fruits, yogurt and other dairy products, eggs, nuts, seeds, and legumes. Pediatricians and nutritionists agree that a semi-vegetarian diet (a lacto-ovo diet containing milk products and eggs) fulfills all of your growing baby's nutritional requirements.

Summary Schedule for Introduction of Foods During Baby's First Year

Best First Foods for Baby	Best Foods for the Beginning Eater	Foods for Baby 6 Months or Older	Foods for Baby 7 Months or Older
Ripe avocado Ripe banana Iron-fortified infant rice cereal Cooked, puréed sweet potatoes	Single grain iron-fortified commercial infant cereals: Barley Millet Oatmeal Whole-milk yogurt (for babies older than 6 months) Cooked, strained fruits: Apricots Nectarines Peaches Pears Plums Prunes	Homemade whole grain cereals: Brown rice Millet Oat Raw mild fruits: Mango Papaya Pears Winter squash	Homemade mixed cereals Cottage cheese Hard-cooked egg Peaches Cooked, puréed: Asparagus Carrots Green beans Peas Summer squash White potatoes Diluted, strained, mild fruit juices: Apple Apricot Grape Papaya Pear Peach Prune Maybe orange juice
Mix finely puréed food with enough liquid until it pours off the spoon into baby's mouth. Food should be only slightly thicker than breast milk/formula.		Food should still be puréed or mashed until it is a smooth and lump-free consistency. Food can be slightly thicker than for beginners— the consistency of thick cream.	

Please remember to verify this schedule with your pediatrician.

Summary Schedule for Introduction of Foods During Baby's First Year (cont.)

Foods for Baby 8 Months or Older	Foods for Baby 9 Months or Older	Foods for Baby 10 Months or Older	Foods for Baby One Year or Older
Tahini	Dried beans, lentils, split peas, ground and cooked	Peanut butter, thinned and creamy (not chunky)	Cow's milk
Ground nuts			Citrus fruits
Ground seeds	Pineapple	Other thinned nut butters	Citrus fruit juices
Nutritional yeast	Brussels sprouts	Homemade bulgur cereal	Tomatoes
Powdered kelp	Cauliflower		Tomato juice
Tofu	Spinach	Cooked whole grain cornmeal with the germ	Hard-cooked egg
Natural cheeses	Beets		Honey
	Kale	Whole grain pasta	
Wheat germ (ask pediatrician permission)	Eggplant		Strawberries, blueberries, and other berries (not whole; cut into small pieces)
	Rhubarb	Ground sprouts	
Apricot	Rutabaga	Finely grated, raw:	
Apple	Turnips	Summer squash	
Cantaloupe		Carrots	
Honeydew	Finely chopped raw parsley	Greens	
Kiwi fruit		Sweet peppers	
Plums	Cooked greens		
Watermelon			
	Cooked onion		
Peeled/quartered grapes (not whole grapes)			
Broccoli			
Okra			
Cooked parsley			
Gradually increase thickness, then chunkiness of food. Offer bite-sized pieces of soft finger foods. Watch very carefully for choking or gagging.		Foods should still be fork-mashed or puréed. Never leave your baby alone while eating.	

Baby and Feeding Safety

Always Consult with Your Pediatrician

Be sure to discuss your baby's diet with your pediatrician, and remember that if her advice and mine conflict, follow her advice. New knowledge about diet and nutrition is constantly being discovered. Your pediatrician will have the latest information on what is best for your baby.

The Four-Day Wait Rule

Introduce only one new food at a time. After you introduce your baby to a new food, do not introduce another new food for at least four days and watch carefully for signs of allergies.

Note: Some experts recommend a three-day waiting period, some recommend waiting five days, and still others recommend a full week of waiting between new foods. Consult with your pediatrician and follow his recommendation.

What to Do If Baby Has an Allergic Reaction
If your baby is having a serious reaction, call 911 immediately!
Inform your pediatrician. If your baby has a small reaction to a particular food, such as a runny nose, your doctor will probably suggest that you try feeding your baby that food again a month later. If he still shows sensitivity, wait to try again until he is at least one year old. Of course, if your baby has a serious reaction, you should not feed your baby that food culprit again.

Recipes for Your Super Baby

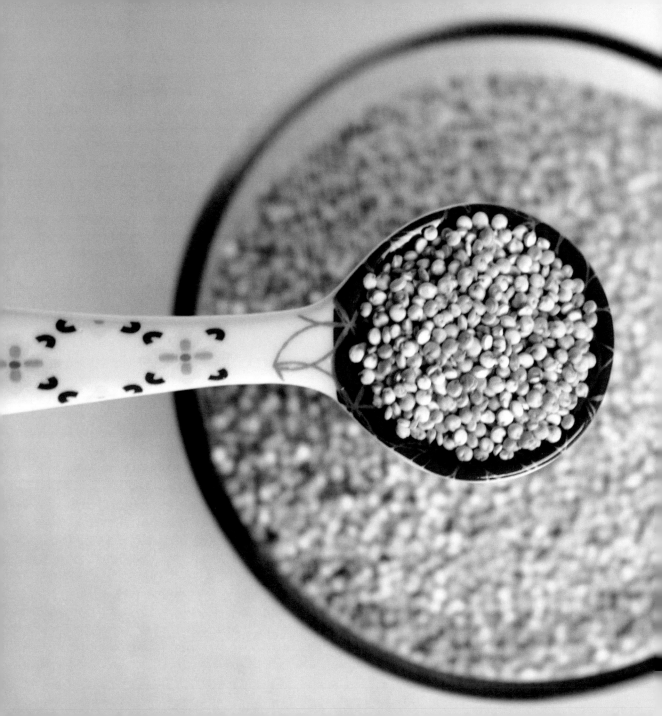

Super Porridge

The first main meal as your baby starts solids is based on *Super Porridge*. *Super Porridge* is a great base for mixtures to which dozens of other foods can be added, from puréed fruits and veggies to wheat germ and ground nuts/seeds. Millet is a super healthy whole grain cereal for your baby, and can be used instead of rice as a first cereal. Like rice, it is not likely to cause allergy and is easily digested. *Super Porridge* can also be made from combinations of different cereal grains (rice, millet, barley, oatmeal, etc.) and legumes (soybeans, split peas, lentils, kidney beans, etc.). So *Super Porridge* is actually a large variety of foods, even though you cook it the same way no matter what grain and legume you choose — the possibilities are endless.

As your baby gets older, the *Super Baby Food Diet* expands with offerings of fruits, vegetables, yogurt, tofu, nuts, seeds, spices and healthy extras such as nutritional yeast and wheat germ. It is an exciting time for you and your baby.

Single Grain Super Porridge

¼ cup brown rice (organic, if possible)
1 cup water

1. Measure 1 cup of water and place into a pot on the stove to boil.

2. Pour rice into your blender. Grind well, for about 2 minutes. (It's going to be very loud, but it's important to let the blender grind the rice down.) If you have a coffee grinder, you may find it works better than a blender. Do not use a food processor, as it does not grind grains well.

3. When the water starts to boil on the stove, turn the heat down to the lowest setting.

4. Sprinkle the ground rice into the water while stirring briskly with a wire whisk.

5. Cover the pot and simmer on low heat for about 10 minutes.

6. Whisk frequently to prevent scorching and to remove lumps.

7. Let cool.

8. Adjust the consistency with some breast milk or formula.

Healthy Extra Tip: For an added nutritional boost, sprinkle a teaspoon of nutritional yeast. (6 months+)

Oatmeal Super Porridge

¼ cup rolled oats or oat groats
1 cup of water

1. Place a cup of water on the stove to boil.
2. While water is heating put rolled oats or oat groats in the blender and grind to a fine powder, approximately 2 minutes.
3. Whisk the oat powder into the water and let it simmer over low heat for 10 minutes, whisking frequently to prevent lumps.
4. Add breast milk or formula to reach the appropriate consistency for your baby and serve.

Millet Super Porridge

3 tablespoons millet
2 cups water

1. Ground millet into fine powder in blender.
2. Bring water to a boil and then reduce heat to lowest setting.
3. Sprinkle the powder into the water and stir with a wire whisk and let it simmer over low heat for 10 minutes, whisking frequently.
4. Adjust the consistency with some breast milk or formula.

Quinoa Super Porridge

1 cup quinoa   2 cups water

1. Grind quinoa in blender until it becomes a fine powder.
2. Bring water to a boil.
3. Sprinkle the powder into boiling water, reduce heat to low and cook for 10 minutes.
4. Whisk throughout the cooking process to prevent lumps.
5. Add breast milk or formula to achieve desired consistency

Variation: Cook the quinoa whole and then blend to desired consistency.

Healthy Extra Tip: Mix the quinoa porridge with fruit, vegetables, or yogurt. (8 months+)

Legume Super Porridge

⅓ cup brown rice, organic, whole kernel (or millet or oatmeal)
⅛ cup dried lentils   2 cups water

1. Ground brown rice and lentils in blender to a fine powder.
2. Bring two cups of water to a boil.
3. Sprinkle the fine powder into the water while stirring with a wire whisk.
4. Reduce heat to low and cook for 10 minutes, stirring frequently.
5. Adjust the consistency with some breast milk or formula.

Healthy Extra Tip: Try mixing with applesauce and sprinkle with wheat germ. (11-12 months)

Purées!

Purée Fruit Basics

Place whole fruit, complete with skin (think nectarine, peach, apple, pear) in boiling water for approximately 45 seconds. Remove the whole fruit with a slotted spoon and into a bowl filled with a few ice cubes and some cold water (an ice water bath.) The skins should be easy to remove with fingers or a paring knife. Once skinned, remove the pit or seeds and cube the reminder of the fruit. Save the water in which the fruit was cooked for later use.

Place the cubed fruit into your blender with a bit of the reserved liquid. Since fruit has a lot of liquid anyway, you might not need to add much reserved water. Purée away! Once blended put the puréed fruit through the holes of a strainer to remove small seeds and any bits of remaining peel.

The recipes that follow will give you ideas for beginner baby foods. The variations are endless. Once you get the hang of it you can easily create your own. I encourage you to share your creations on our website at www.superbabyfood.com.

Banana Smash

Talk about handy, bananas are nutritious and versatile—
when the time is right you can add many goodies to it.

1. Peel a ripe banana.
2. Fork mash or purée in your blender.
3. Adjust the consistency with some breast milk or formula.

Healthy Extra Tip: For an added nutritional boost, add a teaspoon of organic coconut oil. (6 months+)

Avocado Smash

Avocado is a terrific first food for baby!

1. Take a sharp knife and cut avocado in half crosswise.
2. Remove the huge seed.
3. Use a spoon to scoop out flesh from peel and place on a flat dish.
4. Use a fork to mash flesh on dish.
5. Adjust the consistency with some breast milk or formula.

Puréed Avocado and Banana with Coconut Oil

1 avocado, peeled and pitted
1 small banana, peeled
1 tablespoon coconut oil (6+ months)
¼ - ½ cup of water

Blend all ingredients in a blender or food processor until smooth.

Healthy Extra Tip: Sprinkle with some wheat germ. (8+ months)

Puréed Cooked Pears or Peaches

1. Select firm, plump pears, or slightly soft peaches. Rinse well.
2. Place fruit in a pot of boiling water for 45 seconds.
3. Remove from pot with a slotted spoon and put into an ice bath.
4. Remove peels with fingers or a paring knife.
5. Remove seeds or pit and cube the remaining fruit.
6. Place fruit cubes in blender and purée away!
7. Add a bit of liquid to achieve desired consistency.
8. Push purée through strainer to remove any seeds and/or peels.

Healthy Extra Tip: Mix puréed peach and/or pear with whole, full fat, plain yogurt. (6-7 months)

Blueberry Purée

2 cups blueberries (fresh or frozen)
1 cup water

1. Put water in a pan and bring to boil.
2. Add blueberries and reduce heat.
3. Simmer for 15-20 minutes; blueberries should be soft and tender.
4. Remove blueberries from pan using a slotted spoon and transfer directly to a blender or processor.
5. Purée away.
6. Freeze any leftovers.

Puréed Cantaloupe

1. Cut cantaloupe flesh into cubes. Make sure to remove all seeds and rind.

2. Steam cantaloupe pieces for approximately 5 minutes or until soft.

3. Reserve leftover liquid.

4. Purée fruit cubes with reserved liquid until desired consistency.

Purée Vegetable Basics

Purées are all the rage and thank goodness. With just a few tips under your belt, you can prepare your baby food using organic, delicious vegetables and here is the best part—you will know exactly what is in the food you give your baby! I will use the term "processor" to refer to your blender, your food processor, your food mill, or whatever you are using to purée. To get the correct liquid consistency necessary for beginner eaters, water must be added to the food mixture being processed.

For most vegetables, use the water in which they were cooked, whether the water is from steaming, baking, or boiling. This water contains valuable nutrients that have leached out of the vegetables during cooking.

Place chunks of cooked vegetables into the bowl of the processor so that it is almost full. Make sure you leave some head room. Add a tablespoon or two of the cooking water. Cover, keep your hand on the lid, and start the processor. Pour water very slowly through the hole in the top of the processer until the food moves freely. Use the least amount of water necessary to get the consistency you need for your baby's age.

Puréed Cooked Sweet Potato

1. Wash sweet potato by scrubbing gently.
2. Steam whole sweet potato for 30 or more minutes or,
3. Place potato in a pot of boiling water on the stove and cover for 20-30 minutes or until tender.
4. Drain boiling water (save a bit of the liquid) and drop potato into a bowl of cold water; the peels will slip right off.
5. Cut cooked potato into quarters.
6. Place pieces into blender or processor with a bit of the reserved liquid.
7. Make sure there are no fibers left in the purée, as they are choking hazards. (A mixer is sometimes better with a larger potato because the fibers stick to the beaters.)
8. Add liquid (breast milk or formula) for desired consistency.

Healthy Extra Tip: For an added nutritional boost, grind a tablespoon of chia seeds and sprinkle immediately onto prepared baby food. (8 months+)

Puréed Cooked Carrots

1. Select small to medium sized carrots that are firm.
2. Wash thoroughly and peel.
3. Cut off and discard the ends.
4. Cut into uniform pieces.
5. Steam pieces for 20 minutes or until tender, reserving the liquid.
6. Place pieces in blender with some reserved liquid. Purée away!

Healthy Extra Tip: Grind a tablespoon of chia seeds, or sprinkle on a bit of wheat germ for a nutritious boost. (8 months+)

Puréed Cooked Broccoli

1. Select medium bunches with small, tightly closed green buds.

2. Wash thoroughly.

3. Cut stems off so that only the florets remain.

4. Steam broccoli florets for 8-10 minutes or until tender, reserving the liquid.

5. Place pieces in blender with some reserved liquid. Purée away!

Healthy Extra Tip: Try mixing the broccoli puree with smashed avocado. (10-11 months)

Puréed Cooked Cauliflower

1. Select clean, creamy white cauliflower.
2. Wash thoroughly.
3. Cut so that only the florets remain.
4. Steam florets, 10 minutes or until tender, reserving the liquid.
5. Place pieces in blender with some reserved liquid.
6. Purée away!

Puréed Cooked Kale

1. Select kale that is loose and not in plastic bags.
2. Wash each leaf under cold water.
3. Discard unwanted leaves.
4. Remove stems.
5. Steam leaves for 5 minutes.
6. Drain the leaves, reserving the liquid.
7. Place pieces in blender with some reserved liquid. Purée away!

Healthy Extra Tip: Kale has a very strong flavor; try adding smashed banana. (11-12 months)

Recipes for Your Super Toddler Breakfast

Syrup Alternatives

Imitation maple syrup sold in supermarkets is nothing more than corn syrup and caramel coloring. Serve real maple syrup, even though it's expensive. Another nice topping for pancakes is fruit jelly—use a brand that contains no added sugar and is all fruit. Liquefy it by adding a bit of water and maybe maple syrup or honey or melted butter/oil. Create a selection of flavored syrups by adding a few tablespoons of different jellies or jams to separate containers of maple syrup. This is a good way to use the last bit of jelly left in the jar—heat the jar a little and the jelly will come right out. Try plain applesauce, or a purée of banana with applesauce, using some added apple juice or water to thin it. Or, make your own syrup with fresh fruit: Blend fresh fruit and a little water or juice in the blender. You can buy fruit syrups at the natural foods store, but you can make your own, too. Yogurt makes a nice base for a pancake syrup. Add a couple of tablespoons of frozen concentrated orange juice, honey, or other sweetener and/or jam and/or a few drops of vanilla or almond extract. Cooked prunes and yogurt (2 tablespoons yogurt per prune) makes a delicious pancake spread. Add some blackstrap molasses to any syrup as a nutritional enhancer, but go light with it because it has a strong taste. Sprinkle some fresh strawberry or banana pieces over the pancakes for an extra special touch. Serve syrup warmed on the stove for extra flavor and to prevent cooling the pancakes.

Cinnamon Oatmeal

1 cup water
⅓ cup raisins
½ cup rolled oats
¼ teaspoon vanilla
½ teaspoon cinnamon
2 tablespoons tahini

In saucepan, bring water and raisins to a boil. Slowly stir in oats. Lower heat. Add vanilla and cinnamon and let cook for 10 minutes. Mix in tahini.

Easy Homemade Granola

Preheat oven to 350°.

Spread 5 cups oats in a 9 x 13-inch pan and heat in oven for 10 minutes.

Meanwhile, combine in a bowl:

⅓ *cup vegetable oil or butter*
½ *cup honey*
1 teaspoon vanilla
1 cup coconut, sweetened or unsweetened
½ *cup well-chopped nuts (almonds are good)*
½ *cup toasted wheat germ*
1 teaspoon cinnamon

Mix into pan with oatmeal and bake for an additional 30 minutes, stirring frequently for even browning. After mixture cools, add:

1½ cups dried fruit (raisins, etc.)
½ *cup sunflower seeds*

Keep refrigerated in a tightly covered container.

Kiwi Health Cereal

1 kiwi fruit, peeled
1 cup cottage cheese
½ teaspoon wheat germ
honey or maple syrup

Dice or mash a kiwi with fork. Add cottage cheese, wheat germ, and a little honey or maple syrup to taste.

Healthy Extra Tip: The vitamin C in the kiwi works well with the calcium in the cottage cheese and the iron in the wheat germ.

Healthy Extra Tip: Add a pinch or two of brewer's yeast (whose bitter flavor will be hidden by the sweetness of the kiwi and honey) for an extra nutritional punch.

Variation: Instead of kiwi, you can use banana; instead of cottage cheese, you can use yogurt or yogurt cheese. Banana adds iron, but not much vitamin C, so serve with orange juice or some other high vitamin C juice.

Super Flour

To make one cup of Super Flour, place the following ingredients into a one-cup dry measuring cup:

1 tablespoon soy flour
1 tablespoon wheat germ
1 teaspoon nutritional yeast

Top off the cup with whole wheat flour to fill the balance of the cup.

Wonderful Waffles

Separate 2 eggs. Mix in this order:

2 beaten egg yolks
1¾ cups milk
2 cups Super Flour
1 tablespoon plus 1 teaspoon baking powder
½ cup melted butter/oil

Beat egg whites until soft peaks form. Fold into other ingredients. Bake in preheated waffle iron until steam stops and waffles are golden brown.

Tip: I use oil-spray or a butter spray and spray the waffle iron between waffles.

Variations: Add 1 shredded apple or a 1 cup frozen blueberries (no need to thaw) or other berries.

Basic Whole Grain Pancakes

Mix in this order:

> *2 cups Super Flour* (see page 57)
> *2 teaspoons baking soda or baking powder*
> *2 lightly beaten eggs*
> *2 cups milk*
> *2 tablespoons oil or melted butter*
> *Healthy Extras* (see page 148) *or some pieces of fruit to make a smiley face*

Don't over-beat the batter, stop stirring once the ingredients are moist (a few lumps are OK) or your pancakes will be tough. Adjust batter by diluting with milk or other liquid if too thick and adding flour if too thin. Heat griddle or skillet until hot. Its temperature is just right when a few drops of cold water dropped on the griddle will jump and sizzle. If the griddle is not hot enough, the water will just lie there and boil; if it is too hot, it will instantaneously evaporate. To prevent pancakes from sticking, add butter/oil after frying pan is hot. Pour a small amount (about 2-3 tablespoons) of batter onto the griddle until the pancake is the size you want. Make even smaller pancakes for your little ones. Cook about 2 to 3 minutes or until the surface is filled with bubbles and the underside is slightly brown. Raise the edge of the pancake with the spatula to test if it is firm and brown. If so, flip and cook the other side 1 to 2 minutes more. Do not flip again or the pancake will be tough. Do NOT use the spatula to press down the pancake (even though it feels so right to do this, doesn't it?) or it will be heavy.

Banana-Oat Blender Pancakes

2 cups oats
1¼ cups vanilla almond milk
1 large ripe, banana
½ teaspoon ground cinnamon
1 heaping tablespoon honey
¼ teaspoon sea salt
1 teaspoon vanilla extract
1½ teaspoons baking powder
1 large egg
coconut oil

Place all ingredients, except egg and coconut oil in the base of a blender and blend until smooth. Add egg and pulse a few times until egg is fully incorporated.

Heat a griddle or large sauté pan over medium heat and melt a teaspoon or two of coconut oil. When hot, pour or scoop the batter onto the griddle, using approximately ¼ cup for each pancake. Brown on both sides (about 2-3 minutes per side) and serve hot with maple syrup.

If batter becomes too thick to pour easily, add 1-2 tablespoons of almond milk to thin to desired consistency.

Great Pumpkin Pancakes

1 beaten egg
1 cup canned pumpkin
2 tablespoons blackstrap molasses
½ cup Super Flour (see page 57)
½ teaspoon baking powder
½ teaspoon pumpkin pie spice

Mix in all ingredients in a bowl and cook as you would regular pancakes. Top with a mixture of yogurt and orange juice, blended to the consistency of syrup.

French Toast Sticks

Beat together:

> *2 eggs*
> *½ cup apple juice OR milk*
> *½ teaspoon vanilla*

Pour mixture on small cookie sheet. Tear 2-3 slices of whole grain bread into pieces or sticks. Place the pieces in the mixture and wait until they completely soak up the liquid. Cook thoroughly on stove top in a greased or oil-sprayed pan so that none of the egg remains raw. Serve immediately.

Eggie in the Middle

Take a piece of whole wheat toast and cut a heart shape (or any other shape) out of the middle. Place it in a greased or spray-oiled non-stick fry pan. Take a spatula and flatten the bread down, especially at the rim edge of the circle. Flip the bread and pour an egg into its middle. You can use a scrambled egg, or if your child likes sunny-side up eggs, pour the egg directly from the shell into the hole in the bread. The egg won't run into the bread if you firmed up the edges of the shape with the spatula. If scrambled, flip the bread and egg with the spatula to cook the other side. If sunny-side up, reduce heat and cook until egg is done.

Egg McHealthy Muffin

Preheat oven to 450°. For each muffin, split a whole grain English muffin and place cut side up on an oil-sprayed baking sheet. For each muffin, beat together in a bowl:

1 egg
2 tablespoons of shredded cheese (cheddar is good)
A little parsley, oregano, basil, or other fresh herbs or
¼ teaspoon dried herbs for each muffin
A pinch of powdered kelp or salt
A pinch of pepper

Place mixed ingredients on muffin and bake for 5-10 minutes.

Lunch and Dinner

Easy One-Dish Casserole

½ cup uncooked lentils
¼ cup soy grits
½ cup whole grains (millet, brown rice, etc.)
1 small chopped onion
3 cups vegetable broth
1 tablespoon parsley
½ teaspoon sweet basil
¼ teaspoon oregano
¼ teaspoon thyme
1 teaspoon garlic powder
¼ - ½ cup shredded mozzarella or cheddar cheese

Preheat oven to 300°.

Combine all ingredients, except cheese, in a covered casserole dish.

Cover and bake for 90 minutes. For final 15 minutes of baking, uncover and top with shredded cheese.

Kale-Rice Casserole

Preheat oven to 325°.

2 cups cooked brown rice or other grain
1 bunch raw kale, washed and chopped
½ cup shredded cheddar cheese
¼ cup fresh parsley
2 beaten eggs

Mix above ingredients and press into greased baking dish.
Top with this mixture:

¼ cup whole wheat bread crumbs
¼ cup wheat germ
3 tablespoons melted butter/oil
¼ cup Parmesan cheese

Bake, uncovered 40 minutes.

Millet Loaf

½ cup chopped onion
1½ cups cooked millet
2 cups cooked lentils
2 cups coarsely chopped greens (spinach is good)

Preheat oven to 350°.

Sauté onion in 4 tablespoons melted butter or oil for one minute. Add chopped greens and cook for another 2 minutes. Add millet and lentils.

Add:

2 beaten eggs
2 medium apples, grated
1 tablespoon lemon juice
1 tablespoon parsley, fresh

Scrape mixture into oiled loaf pan and bake 35-40 minutes.

Apricot Burgers

In blender or processor, finely chop separately:

> *3 dried apricots*
> *½ medium carrot, grated*
> *2 tablespoons ground nuts*

Mix above thoroughly with:

> *1½ cups cooked brown rice, bulgur or other whole grain*
> *¼ cup raisins*

In blender, process together until smooth:

> *1½ tablespoons tahini*
> *2 tablespoons maple syrup*
> *¼ cup firm tofu*

Mix all ingredients together. Shape into 4-5 adult-sized or 6-8 child-sized patties. Dredge patties in whole grain bread crumbs (*see page 147*), if desired. Broil on each side on lightly oiled baking sheet in oven, or on outdoor grill, until heated through and browned.

Rice Burgers

1 cup brown rice
3 tablespoons minced onion
2 tablespoons chopped green peppers
3 tablespoons chopped celery
1 beaten egg
¼ rolled oats
¼ cup wheat germ
1-2 tablespoons Super Flour (see page 57)

Mix all ingredients except Super Flour. Add enough Super Flour until you've achieved a good consistency to make patties. Dust with more wheat germ, then sauté on both sides in a little butter or olive oil. Optionally, melt a slice of cheese on top of each patty. Makes 8 adult-sized or twice as many or more toddler-sized patties.

Avocado Soy Patties

1 medium avocado, mashed
1 cup cooked soybeans, mashed
¼ cup cooked brown rice
½ cup minced raw onion
1 tablespoon prepared mustard
1 tablespoon tomato paste
2 tablespoons wheat germ

Mix all ingredients and add enough whole wheat bread crumbs *(see page 147)* until you can form into patties. Sauté patties on both sides in a little butter or oil until browned.

Broccoli Cheese Rice Quiche

Crust

Preheat oven to 425°. Mix

2 cups cooked brown rice
1½ ounces of grated cheese
1 beaten egg

Pat into greased pie tin. Bake for 15 minutes.

Filling

Reduce heat in oven to 350°.
Arrange in bottom of crust:

1 cup cooked chopped broccoli florets
1 cup shredded natural cheese (Swiss and mozzarella are good)

In separate bowl, mix:

4 beaten eggs
1½ cups milk

Pour over broccoli and bake until firm.
Let stand 15 minutes before serving.

Eggplant Parmesan

Dry ingredients:

¼ cup *Super Flour* (see page 57)
1 tablespoon Parmesan cheese
1 tablespoon wheat germ
1 tablespoon whole grain bread crumbs (see page 147)
1 teaspoon dried parsley

Wet ingredients:

1 tablespoon milk   *1 beaten egg*

1 eggplant   *Tomato sauce*   *Shredded mozzarella cheese*

Preheat oven to 350°.

In a shallow bowl, mix dry ingredients, which will make approximately ½ cup. In another bowl, mix wet ingredients.

Slice one raw eggplant into ¼-½ inch slices. Moisten both sides of each slice by dipping in wet ingredients. Then dip into bowl of dry ingredients to coat each side with flour mixture.

Grease a large baking pan. Layer slices of eggplant into the pan. Cover each layer with tomato sauce and sprinkle with Parmesan cheese. Cover the pan tightly and bake 35-45 minutes, or until eggplant is tender when pierced with fork. Turn off the oven. Sprinkle top with shredded mozzarella cheese and return pan to oven. Let sit for 5 to 10 minutes until mozzarella is nicely melted.

Tofu Lasagna Roll Ups

8 whole wheat lasagna noodles
2½ cups tomato sauce
2 cups shredded mozzarella cheese
1 cup mashed tofu
¼ cup grated Parmesan cheese

Cook lasagna noodles according to directions on package and then rinse under cold water.

Preheat oven to 350°.

Combine tofu and Parmesan cheese in a bowl.

On each cooked noodle, spread a thin layer of the tofu mixture and about 2 tablespoons of tomato sauce, then sprinkle with some shredded cheese. Roll up the noodle jelly-roll style and place it on its side in the baking pan so that you can see the spiral from the top view. When finished with all the noodles, pour the rest of the sauce over them and sprinkle with the rest of the mozzarella cheese. Bake, covered, for 30-45 minutes. Freeze leftovers.

Tip: You may wish to cut the noodles in half to make them shorter, so that the spirals will be toddler size.

Variation: Create an additional layer by adding 1 cup chopped baby spinach.

Fried Rice

¼ cup of finely chopped onions
1 cup cooked brown rice
⅓ cup cooked green peas
1 beaten egg

Sauté onions in 1 tablespoon of butter or olive oil. Remove from pan. Add more butter/oil to pan and sauté brown rice. Add green peas and egg and continue to sauté until egg is cooked through. You can double or triple this recipe.

Variation: Replace some onion with minced green peppers and/or celery.

Pineapple Brown Rice

1 cup brown rice
1½ cups water
½ cup pineapple juice

Bring water and pineapple juice to boil. Add brown rice and cook according to directions on brown rice (substituting ½ cup pineapple juice for ½ cup water). When rice has finished cooking, stir in:

1 cup yogurt
1 can drained pineapple chunks or crushed pineapple
½ cup ground nuts (and/or seeds if you're going to eat it immediately)

Variation: Use another whole grain instead of brown rice and, of course, adjust water and pineapple juice amounts proportionately.

Cheesy Mashed Cauliflower

2 cups cooked cauliflower (and/or broccoli)
3 cups organic cheddar cheese, shredded
2 tablespoons minced parsley, chervil, or other herb (optional)
Small pinch of nutmeg (optional)

Place all ingredients into food processor for a mashed potato-like consistency.

Variation: Add a bit of cooked minced onion and/or garlic for nutrition, flavor, and texture.

Easy Macaroni and Cheese

1 cup cooked whole grain pasta
¼ cup grated natural cheese
¼ cup cottage or ricotta cheese
1 teaspoon butter
2-3 tablespoons of milk

Mix all ingredients. Heat on stove top until cheese and butter melt. Add a sprinkle of wheat germ on top.

Easy Bean Soup

3 cups cooked or canned beans (your favorite kind)
1 cup vegetable broth

Purée 2 cups of beans with broth for a thick and creamy soup base.

Place a cup of whole cooked beans, not puréed, into a medium-sized pot. Add puréed bean soup base. Optionally, add seasonings to taste. Cook over medium heat, stirring frequently, until hot, and serve.

Mr. and Ms. Sweet Potato Heads

Slice 2 cooked sweet potatoes in half. Scoop out flesh, being careful to keep skin intact to be used as a bowl later. Mash flesh and mix with:

2 tablespoons yogurt
1 tablespoon maple syrup or honey
2 tablespoons orange juice

Replace mashed potato mixture into reserved skin bowls. Use your own decorative touches (berries, avocado, etc.) to make eyes, nose, mouth, and hair. Serve to children. For adults, you may have to reheat in the oven.

Variation: Make mashed potato mixture by mixing flesh from the sweet potatoes with ¼-½ cup of puréed pineapple chunks.

Snacks and Desserts

Avocado Cube Salad

My kids loved this as an outdoors summer afternoon snack.

Cut small cubes of avocado and/or banana and/or firm tofu.
Drizzle with a little lemon juice and honey *(about 1 tablespoon per cup of cubes)*.

Avocado Dip

Mix mashed avocado with an equal amount of cottage cheese or tofu. Add Healthy Extras *(see page 148)*, if desired. The avocado skins can be used as cups to hold this dip. Use it for dipping anything from whole-grain breadsticks *(see page 117)* to carrot sticks. Or use as a spread in sandwiches, on whole-grain crackers, celery sticks, or fruit pieces.

Strawberry Pizza

Preheat oven to 350°.
For crust, mix:

> *½ cup wheat germ*
> *½ cup ground oatmeal*
> *1 beaten egg*
> *1 tablespoon melted butter or oil*

Press into bottom of a 9-inch pie plate; don't go up the sides.
Bake for 10 minutes.

For filling, mix:

> *½ cup of yogurt cheese (or cottage cheese)*
> *1 tablespoon of orange juice or other fruit concentrate*

Spread filling on crust.

For topping: Arrange fresh strawberries over filling into a design or shape or letter. Cut with pizza cutter. Keep refrigerated or freeze.

Variation: Replace strawberries with other fruit or use a mixture of fresh fruit.

Canoes for Riding the Rapids

A slightly curved, shorter banana is good for this recipe. Wash the outside of a banana. Make a vertical slit down one side of the unpeeled banana leaving about ½ inch uncut at each end. If the banana is curved, make the slit on the "upside" so that it's shaped like a canoe. Open slit and carefully scoop out the flesh.

Fork-mash half of the banana and mix with ½ cup of mashed tofu, 2 tablespoons of ground seeds, 1 tablespoon of wheat germ, and honey to taste. Spread banana peel open gently and make bottom of canoe flat by pressing with fingers so that it will be stable, being careful not to rip ends.

Return mixture to inside of banana. You can trim around the slit with a sharp knife to make the opening wider.

Use the other half of the banana flesh to shape fish and rocks, roll in wheat germ, and place them around the canoe. These dangerous rocks must be avoided to prevent the canoe from breaking apart.

Make oars out of carrot or celery sticks or anything else handy.

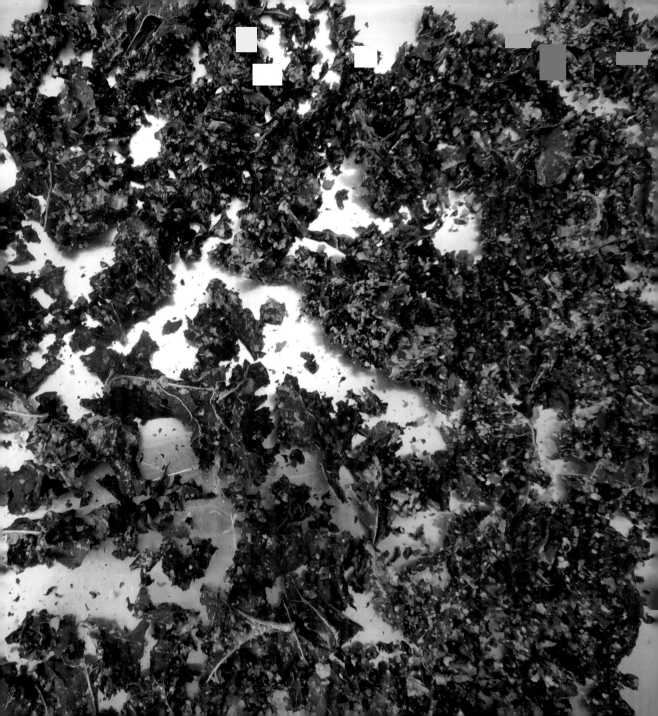

Crispy Kale Chips

Preheat oven to 300°.

Remove the stems from a bunch of kale leaves by folding the leaf in half along the stem line. While holding leaves in your right hand use your left hand to hold the stem on the bottom and rip upwards using your right hand in a quick motion from bottom to top.

Cut the kale leaves into bite-sized pieces.

Spread the kale pieces flat on a cookie sheet.

Sprinkle with olive oil, but be careful not to oversaturate.

Cook at 300° for 15 minutes, then turn the kale leaves on the pan and cook for another 10 to 15 minutes for desired crispiness.

Let sit on the pan for 5 minutes and then sprinkle with seasoning.

Variation: Add a bit of shredded cheese during the last five minutes of cooking.

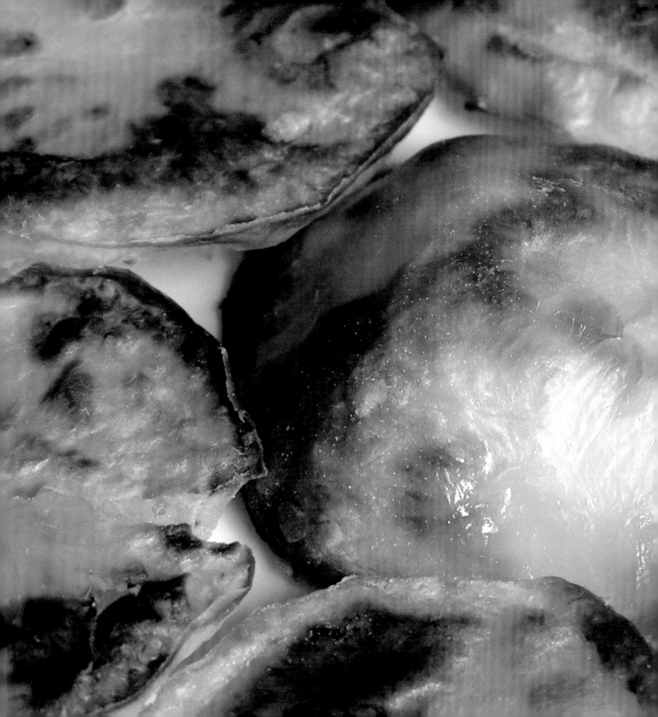

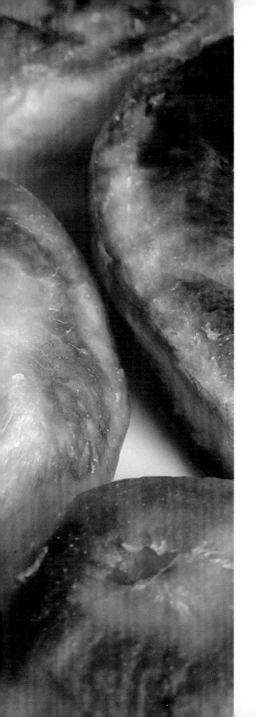

Healthy Potato Chips

Preheat oven to 450°.

Slice well-washed, unpeeled potatoes (about 1 pound) very thin using a food processor or by hand.

Spread one layer of potatoes on a large, oiled cookie sheet. Brush tops with oil.

Bake for 8-10 minutes until lightly browned. Turn cookie sheet halfway through cooking for more even browning.

Shake potato chips, while still warm, in paper lunch bag with seasoning to taste.

Store in cool, dry place in sealed container.

Tofu Fingers

1 package firm tofu, drained
¼ cup melted butter, milk or water
¼ cup whole grain bread crumbs (see page 147)
1 teaspoon wheat germ
1 tablespoon grated Parmesan cheese
pinch of oregano and/or onion powder or garlic powder

Preheat oven to 350°.

Slice tofu into strips.

Combine bread crumbs, wheat germ, Parmesan cheese and oregano and/or onion powder or garlic powder.

Dip tofu strips into melted butter, milk, or water. Dredge in dry ingredients.

Bake on ungreased cookie sheet for 15-20 minutes, turning once.

Quick Breadsticks

Makes about 16 sticks.

Mix the following dry ingredients in a bowl.

> *1 cup Super Flour* (see page 57)
> *½ cup oat or wheat bran*
> *½ teaspoon baking powder*

In another bowl, mix the following wet ingredients.

> *1 beaten egg*
> *4 tablespoons melted butter or olive oil*
> *¼ cup of water*

Preheat oven to 350°.

Make well in dry ingredients and mix in wet ingredients. If dough is too dry, add water; if too wet, add a little more flour or bran. Keep dividing dough in half until you have 16 balls.

Roll balls into sticks about ½ inch in diameter. If desired, combine a beaten egg with 2 tablespoons of water and lightly moisten sticks, then roll them in sesame seeds or wheat germ.

Place on greased baking sheet and bake for 20 minutes, until crisp and golden-brown.

Store in an air-tight container.

Banana Nut Bread

Preheat oven to 350°.

Mix the following wet ingredients in one bowl.

> *1 beaten egg*
> *3 medium ripe bananas, peeled and mashed*
> *3 tablespoons melted butter*
> *3 tablespoons honey*
> *2 tablespoons frozen orange juice concentrate*
> *1 teaspoon vanilla*

Mix the following dry ingredients in another bowl.

> *1½ cups Super Flour (see page 57)*
> *1 teaspoon baking soda*
> *A pinch of salt*

Combine wet ingredients with dry ingredients and add ¾ cup finely chopped nuts (walnuts, filberts, and almonds are good). Pour into loaf pan and bake 50-60 minutes.

Variation: Replace all or some of the nuts with sunflower seeds.

Banana Nut Muffins

Preheat oven to 375°.

Mix the following dry ingredients in large bowl.

>   *1¾ Super Flour (see page 57)*
>   *½ teaspoon baking powder*
>   *½ teaspoon baking soda*
>   *1 teaspoon cinnamon*
>   *½ cup ground walnuts*

Mix the following wet ingredients in small bowl.

>   *2 beaten eggs*
>   *¼ cup yogurt*
>   *2 tablespoons melted butter/oil*
>   *¼ cup maple syrup*
>   *1 tablespoon lemon juice*
>   *3 small mashed ripe bananas (about 1 cup)*
>   *½ cup plumped raisins*

Add wet ingredients to dry ingredients and stir until blended. Pour into greased or lined muffin tins. Decorate each muffin with a walnut on top (not for babies/toddlers—whole nuts are choking hazards). Bake 20 minutes or until golden.

Nut Banana Bites

3-4 ripe peeled bananas
½ cup crushed wheat squares cereal
1 tablespoon peanut butter or other nut butter
1 tablespoon honey
1 teaspoon carob powder

Mash all together and roll into bite-sized balls.

Eggless Apple Muffins

Preheat oven to 350°.

Mix the following dry ingredients in large bowl.

2 cups Super Flour (see page 57)
½ cup rolled oats
2 teaspoons baking powder
1 teaspoon baking soda
½ teaspoon cinnamon

Mix the following ingredients in a small bowl.

3 cups unsweetened applesauce
½ cup yogurt
2 tablespoons molasses
½ cup plumped raisins

Add this mixture into the dry ingredients in the large bowl and stir to blend well. Pour into greased or lined muffin cups. Decorate with ground nuts, if desired. Bake 25-30 minutes.

Apple Smiley Face

1 apple (peeled and cored)
1 tablespoon peanut or other butter
1 teaspoon honey or maple syrup or blackstrap molasses (optional)
1 pinch ground cinnamon or nutmeg

Grate the apple in a food processor.

Mix with 1 tablespoon of peanut butter or other nut butter.

Add 1 teaspoon honey, maple syrup or blackstrap molasses and a pinch of cinnamon and/or nutmeg, if desired.

Add Healthy Extras *(see page 148)*—grated carrots are good.

Place on small plate and form into pancake-shaped face. Use berries or other fruit for your own decorative touches to create eyes, nose, hair, etc.

Mock Ice Cream

Purée frozen bananas (peeled) in blender or food processor. Add orange juice, honey, and/or vanilla to taste.

Homemade Ice Cream Sandwiches

Make your own ice cream sandwiches by placing Mock Ice Cream, frozen ice cream, or yogurt between two large, flat homemade cookies. Freeze until solid.

Mock Whipped Cream

Following are healthy alternatives to the expensive supermarket whipped cream products, which have lots of sugar and preservatives.

Mock Whipped Cream I

1 cup cottage cheese
1 tablespoon unsweetened pineapple concentrate
1 tablespoon lemon concentrate

Process ingredients in a blender at high speed until peaks form.
Serve immediately.

Mock Whipped Cream II

Add equivalent of one pasteurized egg white to a thoroughly mashed banana. Use an electric mixer and beat until mixture stands in peaks. Add ½ teaspoon vanilla and 1 tablespoon honey or other sweetener. If you wish, add coloring.

Mock Whipped Cream III

Put one cup ice water in your blender. Slowly mix in one cup nonfat dry milk and blend until consistency of whipped cream—about 5 minutes. Serve immediately.

Mock Whipped Cream Tips

Tip: Poke beaters through a sheet of wax paper before inserting into mixer base. The wax paper covering the bowl will help prevent messy splatters.

Tip: To whip a small amount of cream, use a sturdy cup and only one beater of your electric mixer. As always, make sure the ingredients, cup, and beater all very cold for better whipping. For sweetened topping, confectioners' sugar makes more fluff than granulated. Evaporated milk will whip, but with more work than heavy cream with its high fat content. For best results, freeze milk in ice cube tray until ice crystals just begin to form. Using an ice cube tray will allow the center of the milk to get colder then a bowl would.

Tip: For a special touch that requires only a few seconds, sprinkle whipped topping on desserts with a little powder that has color: cinnamon, carob or cocoa powder, nutmeg, powdered kelp, etc.

Creamy Fruit Slushy

½ cup unsweetened apple juice or any fruit juice
½ cup low-fat plain yogurt
1 teaspoon maple syrup or blackstrap molasses
2 ice cubes

Blend all ingredients very well, adding more ice or water to desired consistency.

Variation: Instead of juice, you can add fruit pieces, such as strawberries, bananas, or blueberries. Or you can add re-hydrated dried fruit, such as papaya and apricots.

Creamy Green Yogurt Smoothie

1 cup organic plain or vanilla Greek yogurt
1 handful chopped, fresh well-washed kale, spinach, or other leafy greens
1 large fresh mango, peeled and stone removed
1 avocado, peeled and stone removed

Put all ingredients in a blender and blend until smooth.

Peanut Butter Pudding

1 small mashed banana
½ cup plain or vanilla yogurt or tofu
½ cup natural peanut butter
1 teaspoon maple syrup or honey
¼ teaspoon vanilla

Mix ingredients in a blender. Process until smooth, pour into individual cups, and refrigerate until cold.

Variation: Replace all or part of the peanut butter or tofu with tahini, almond butter, or other nut/seed butters.

Chia Pudding

½ cup chia seeds
2 cups water

Mix ½ cup chia seeds into 2 cups water and let soak. After about 45 minutes, the seeds will have absorbed all the water and be similar to tapioca. After soaking, there will be about 2 cups. You can add any flavorings you want.

Variation: Instead of using water as the liquid, you can use almond or coconut milk, or juice.

Variation: Divide pudding into four custard cups and stir in a teaspoon of maple syrup and raw cacao or carob to each custard cup for chocolate pudding.

Variation: Blend 1 teaspoon vanilla extract and 2 Medjool dates in the blender. Add to pudding.

Coconut Milk Chia Seed Pudding

3 tablespoons black chia seeds
¾ cup unsweetened coconut milk
1 teaspoon vanilla
1 sprinkle ground cinnamon
¾ cup raspberries

In a bowl, mix chia seeds, coconut milk, vanilla, and cinnamon.

Let sit for 15 minutes or refrigerate overnight.

Add raspberries or other colorful fruit when set.

Super Milks

Super Milks are super nutritious, but should not decrease your baby's intake of breast milk, formula, or cow's milk, which is your baby/toddler's main source of calcium, vitamin D, and protein. Make sure your baby is getting the recommended amounts of milks. Use Super Milks in addition to regular milk.

Nut Milk

Grind in blender ⅓-½ cup organic nuts to fine powder. Slowly add 1 cup cold water. Good nuts to use are raw cashews and blanched almonds. Blanch almonds by pouring boiling water over almonds, let stand for two minutes, and drain. Remove skins by pressing each almond between your thumb and index finger and popping the nut out of its skin.

Nut/Seed Milk

⅓ cup organic nuts or seeds (cashews, almonds or sesame seeds are good)
1 cup water

Rinse nuts and seeds and let soak in water overnight before blending. This will begin the sprouting process, increase the nutrients in the water, and soften the seeds/nuts for better blending. In the morning, liquefy in blender. Shake well before each use. You can strain this milk, but don't discard the pulp—it's full of nutrients. Use it in adult family members' cereals and salads. The milk will keep in the refrigerator for up to 3 days.

Tip: Use a fine strainer to remove the powdery pulp in blended nut milks. A yogurt strainer works great.

Whole Grain Bread Crumbs

Don't throw away bread crusts and the end slices from whole grain bread. Save them in a paper bag until they get stale and hard. Then break them into small pieces and whiz them in your blender or food processor to make bread crumbs. Store in a tightly-covered jar in your kitchen cabinets. Three slices will make about one cup of crumbs.

Variation: Crush dried bread with a rolling pin to have more control over the coarseness.

Variation: I think they taste fine, but if you find that the bread crumbs taste like stale bread, try drying fresh bread on an ungreased baking sheet in a single layer at 300° in the oven until completely dry and lightly browned. Let cool completely before pulverizing.

Healthy Extras for Super Nutrition Enhancers

Nutritional yeast
Wheat germ
Ground dry oatmeal or rolled oats
Tofu
Yogurt
Cooked crumbled egg
Shredded or diced raw vegetables (carrots, broccoli, celery, cabbage)
Chopped fresh or frozen parsley
Mashed (or whole for babies over 3 years) cooked dried beans or
  frozen puréed cooked bean food cubes
Cooked soy grits
Bean flour
Ground nuts (almonds, walnuts, filberts, etc.)
Nut and seed butters (peanut butter, almond butter, tahini, etc.)
Ground seeds (pumpkin, flax, chia, etc.) Eat immediately
Cooked brown rice or millet grains or any cooked whole grains
Milks: breast, formula, super milks (see page 145), instant non-fat dry milk

These healthy extras can double as sweeteners:
Shredded or diced fresh fruits (apples, pears, kiwi, etc.)
Chopped dried fruits, rehydrated (apricots, papaya, etc.)
Blackstrap molasses
Mashed fresh or mashed frozen strawberries and other berries
Concentrated frozen all-fruit juices
Natural no-added-sugar all-fruit jams or jellies

About the Author

When Ruth Yaron's twin boys were born premature and very sick, she knew the most important thing she could do for them was to feed them the healthiest diet possible. Unhappy with the information that was available to her, Ruth decided to do her own exhaustive research on nutrition and health food. Although she was a whiz at programming satellites for NASA, Ruth was an inexperienced cook. She used dozens of natural cookbooks to learn her way around a kitchen, experimenting with tofu, carob and wheat germ, much to the surprise of friends and family.

A determined mother is a great motivator. She utilized her skills, developed writing technical manuals for the everyday reader, to diligently record her research of homemade, mostly organic, whole grain cereals, fruits, and home-cooked vegetables, as well as the best storing and freezing methods to diligently record her research on homemade, mostly organic, whole grain cereals, fruits, and home-cooked vegetables, as well as the best storing and freezing methods. The result was a remarkably easy and complete system of baby food preparation: **Super Baby Food**.

Nearly three quarters of a million copies of **Super Baby Food** have been sold. Ruth's fans have dubbed the book their "baby food bible" and it has become the quintessential baby and toddler-feeding guide for hundreds of thousands of parents world-wide.

Ruth continues to research and share **Super Baby Food** tips at **www.SuperBabyFood.com**, on Facebook (**www.facebook.com/SuperBabyFood**), Twitter (**@Super_Baby_Food**) and on Instagram (**SuperBabyFood**). She loves to interact with new parents and will answer any of the energetic, insightful questions they have.

Ruth Yaron graduated from East Stroudsburg University in Pennsylvania with degrees in Mathematics and Computer Science. She previously worked at the GE Space Division and programmed satellites for NASA. She is the mother of three sons and lives with her husband in Scranton, Pennsylvania.

Photo Credits